SCHOLASTIC

READ & RESPOND

Bringing the best books to life in the classroom

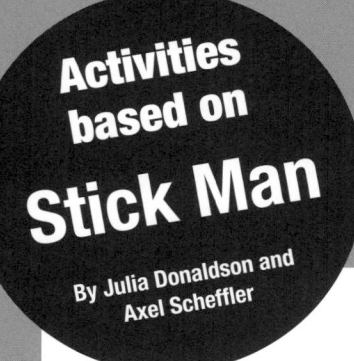

Activities based on **Stick Man**
By Julia Donaldson and Axel Scheffler

Terms and conditions

IMPORTANT – PERMITTED USE AND WARNINGS – READ CAREFULLY BEFORE USING

Copyright in the software contained in this CD-ROM and in its accompanying material belongs to Scholastic Limited. All rights reserved. © 2016 Scholastic Ltd.

Save for these purposes, or as expressly authorised in the accompanying materials, the software may not be copied, reproduced, used, sold, licensed, transferred, exchanged, hired, or exported in whole or in part or in any manner or form without the prior written consent of Scholastic Ltd. Any such unauthorised use or activities are prohibited and may give rise to civil liabilities and criminal prosecutions.

The material contained on this CD-ROM may only be used in the context for which it was intended in *Read & Respond,* and is for use only by the purchaser or purchasing institution that has purchased the book and CD-ROM. Permission to download images is given for purchasers only and not for users from any lending service. Any further use of the material contravenes Scholastic Ltd's copyright and that of other rights holders.

This CD-ROM has been tested for viruses at all stages of its production. However, we recommend that you run virus-checking software on your computer systems at all times. Scholastic Ltd cannot accept any responsibility for any loss, disruption or damage to your data or your computer system that may occur as a result of using either the CD-ROM or the data held on it.

IF YOU ACCEPT THE ABOVE CONDITIONS YOU MAY PROCEED TO USE THE CD-ROM.

Recommended system requirements:
Windows: XP (Service Pack 3), Vista (Service Pack 2), Windows 7 or Windows 8 with 2.33GHz processor
Mac: OS 10.6 to 10.8 with Intel Core™ Duo processor
1GB RAM (recommended)
1024 x 768 Screen resolution
CD-ROM drive (24x speed recommended)
Adobe Reader (version 9 recommended for Mac users)
Broadband internet connections (for installation and updates)

For all technical support queries (including no CD drive), please phone Scholastic Customer Services on 0845 6039091.

Designed using Adobe Indesign
Published by Scholastic Education, an imprint of Scholastic Ltd
Book End, Range Road, Witney, Oxfordshire, OX29 0YD
Registered office: Westfield Road, Southam, Warwickshire CV47 0RA

Printed and bound by Ashford Colour Press
© 2016 Scholastic Ltd
1 2 3 4 5 6 7 8 9   6 7 8 9 0 1 2 3 4 5

British Library Cataloguing-in-Publication Data
A catalogue record for this book is available from the British Library.
ISBN 978-1407-16053-5

All rights reserved. This book is sold subject to the condition that it shall not, by way of trade or otherwise, be lent, hired out or otherwise circulated without the publisher's prior consent in any form of binding or cover other than that in which it is published and without a similar condition, including this condition, being imposed upon the subsequent purchaser.

No part of this publication may be reproduced, stored in a retrieval system, or transmitted, in any form or by any means, electronic, mechanical, photocopying, recording or otherwise, other than for the purposes described in the lessons in this book, without the prior permission of the publisher. This book remains copyright, although permission is granted to copy pages where indicated for classroom distribution and use only in the school which has purchased the book, or by the teacher who has purchased the book, and in accordance with the CLA licensing agreement. Photocopying permission is given only for purchasers and not for borrowers of books from any lending service.

Extracts from *The National Curriculum in England, English Programme of Study* © Crown Copyright. Reproduced under the terms of the Open Government Licence (OGL). http://www.nationalarchives.gov.uk/doc/open-government-licence/version/3

Due to the nature of the web, we cannot guarantee the content or links of any site mentioned. We strongly recommend that teachers check websites before using them in the classroom.

Author Sarah Snashall
Editorial team Rachel Morgan, Jenny Wilcox, Tracy Kewley, Elizabeth Evans
Series designer Neil Salt
Designer Anna Oliwa
Illustrator Gemma Hastilow
Digital development Hannah Barnett, Phil Crothers and MWA Technologies Private Ltd

Acknowledgements
The publishers gratefully acknowledge permission to reproduce the following copyright material:

Scholastic Ltd for the use of the cover, extract text and illustrations from *Stick Man* written by Julia Donaldson and illustrated by Axel Scheffler. Text copyright © Julia Donaldson, 2008, illustration copyright © Axel Scheffler, 2008. Reproduced with the permission of Alison Green Books, an imprint of Scholastic Ltd.

Every effort has been made to trace copyright holders for the works reproduced in this book, and the publishers apologise for any inadvertent omissions.

CONTENTS

Introduction	4
Using the CD-ROM	5
Curriculum links	6
About the book and author	7
Guided reading	8
Shared reading	11
Phonics & spelling	15
Plot, character & setting	17
Talk about it	22
Get writing	26
Assessment	31

INTRODUCTION

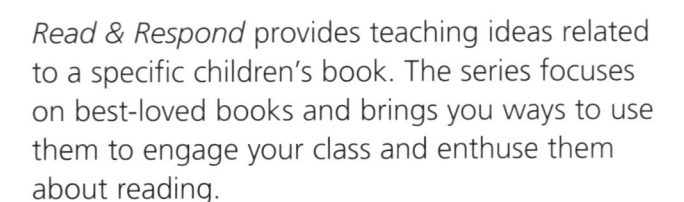

Read & Respond provides teaching ideas related to a specific children's book. The series focuses on best-loved books and brings you ways to use them to engage your class and enthuse them about reading.

The book is divided into different sections:

- **About the book and author:** gives you some background information about the book and the author.
- **Guided reading:** breaks the book down into sections and gives notes for using it with guided reading groups. A bookmark has been provided on page 10 containing comprehension questions. The children can be directed to refer to these as they read.
- **Shared reading:** provides extracts from the children's books with associated notes for focused work. There is also one non-fiction extract that relates to the children's book.
- **Phonics & spelling:** provides phonics and spelling work related to the children's book so you can teach these skills in context.
- **Plot, character & setting:** contains activity ideas focused on the plot, characters and the setting of the story.
- **Talk about it:** has speaking and listening activities related to the children's book. These activities may be based directly on the children's book or be broadly based on the themes and concepts of the story.
- **Get writing:** provides writing activities related to the children's book. These activities may be based directly on the children's book or be broadly based on the themes and concepts of the story.
- **Assessment:** contains short activities that will help you assess whether the children have understood concepts and curriculum objectives. They are designed to be informal activities to feed into your planning.

The activities follow the same format:

- **Objective:** the objective for the lesson. It will be based upon a curriculum objective, but will often be more specific to the focus being covered.
- **What you need:** a list of resources you need to teach the lesson, including digital resources (printable pages, interactive activities and media resources, see page 5).
- **What to do:** the activity notes.
- **Differentiation:** this is provided where specific and useful differentiation advice can be given to support and/or extend the learning in the activity. Differentiation by providing additional adult support has not been included as this will be at a teacher's discretion based upon specific children's needs and ability, as well as the availability of support.

The activities are numbered for reference within each section and should move through the text sequentially – so you can use the lesson while you are reading the book. Once you have read the book, most of the activities can be used in any order you wish.

USING THE CD-ROM

Below are brief guidance notes for using the CD-ROM. For more detailed information, please click on the '?' button in the top right-hand corner of the screen.

The program contains the following:
- the extract pages from the book
- all of the photocopiable pages from the book
- additional printable pages
- interactive on-screen activities
- media resources.

Getting started

Put the CD-ROM into your CD-ROM drive. If you do not have a CD-ROM drive, phone Scholastic Customer Services on 0845 6039091.

- For Windows users, the install wizard should autorun; if it fails to do so then navigate to your CD-ROM drive. Then follow the installation process.
- For Mac users, copy the disk image file to your hard drive. After it has finished copying double click it to mount the disk image. Navigate to the mounted disk image and run the installer. After installation the disk image can be unmounted and the DMG can be deleted from the hard drive.
- To install on a network, see the ReadMe file located on the CD-ROM (navigate to your drive).

To complete the installation of the program you need to open the program and click 'Update' in the pop-up. Please note – this CD-ROM is web-enabled and the content will be downloaded from the internet to your hard drive to populate the CD-ROM with the relevant resources. This only needs to be done on first use; after this you will be able to use the CD-ROM without an internet connection. If at any point any content is updated, you will receive another pop-up upon start up when there is an internet connection.

Main menu

The main menu is the first screen that appears. Here you can access: terms and conditions, registration links, how to use the CD-ROM and credits. To access a specific book click on the relevant button (NB only titles installed will be available). You can filter by the drop-down lists if you wish. You can search all resources by clicking 'Search' in the bottom left-hand corner. You can also log in and access favourites that you have bookmarked.

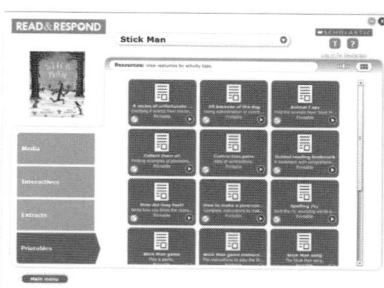

Resources

By clicking on a book on the Main menu, you are taken to the resources for that title. The resources are: Media, Interactives, Extracts and Printables. Select the category and then launch a resource by clicking the play button.

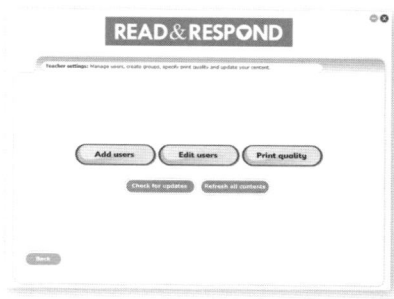

Teacher settings

In the top right-hand corner of the screen is a small 'T' icon. This is the teacher settings area. It is password protected; the password is: login. This area will allow you to choose the print quality settings for interactive activities ('Default' or 'Best') and also allow you to check for updates to the program or re-download all content to the disk via Refresh all content. You can also set up user logins so that you can save and access favourites. Once a user is set up, they can enter by clicking the login link underneath the 'T' and '?' buttons.

Search

You can access an all resources search by clicking the search button on the bottom left of the Main menu. You can search for activities by type (using the drop-down filter) or by keyword by typing into the box. You can then assign resources to your favourites area or launch them directly from the search area.

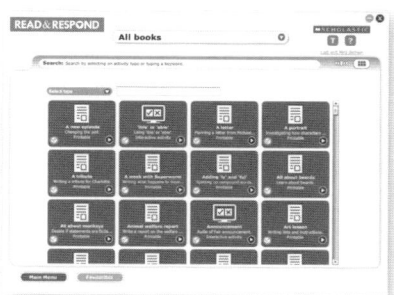

READ&RESPOND Stick Man **5**

CURRICULUM LINKS

Section	Activity	Curriculum objectives
Guided reading		Comprehension: To make inferences on the basis of what is being said and done; to predict what might happen on the basis of what has been read so far; to participate in discussion about what is read to them.
Shared reading	1	Comprehension: To recognise and join in with predictable phrases.
	2	Comprehension: To make inferences on the basis of what is being said and done.
	3	Comprehension: To listen to and discuss non-fiction.
Phonics & spelling	1	Transcription: To spell by segmenting words into phonemes and representing these by graphemes.
	2	Transcription: To add 'ing', 'ed', 'er', and 'est' to a root word.
	3	Transcription: To learn new ways of spelling phonemes.
	4	Transcription: To learn to spell words with contracted forms.
Plot, character & setting	1	Comprehension: To discuss the significance of the title and the events; to discuss the sequence of events in books.
	2	Composition: To use subordination and coordination.
	3	Comprehension: To make inferences on the basis of what is being said and done. Composition: To use subordination and coordination.
	4	Comprehension: To explain what is read to them; to discuss the sequence of events in books.
	5	Comprehension: To draw on what they know and vocabulary provided by the teacher.
	6	Comprehension: To make inferences on the basis of what is being said and done.
Talk about it	1	Spoken language: To give well-structured descriptions, explanations and narratives.
	2	Spoken language: To maintain attention and participate actively in conversations.
	3	Spoken language: To participate in discussions, performances, role play and improvisation.
	4	Spoken language: To participate in performances, role play and improvisations.
	5	Spoken language: To consider and evaluate different viewpoints.
	6	Spoken language: To participate in presentations.
Get writing	1	Composition: To punctuate sentences using a capital letter and a full stop, question mark or exclamation mark; to use sentences with different forms; to use expanded noun phrases.
	2	Composition: To sequence sentences to form short narratives; to write narratives about personal experiences and those of others.
	3	Composition: To write for different purposes; to write ideas and/or key words.
	4	Composition: To write poetry.
	5	Composition: To compose a sentence orally before writing it.
	6	Composition: To re-read what they have written to check it makes sense and that verbs are used correctly and consistently.
Assessment	1	Composition: To learn how to use subordination (using 'when', 'if', 'that' or 'because') and coordination (using 'or', 'and' or 'but').
	2	Transcription: To spell more words with contracted forms.
	3	Composition: To use expanded noun phrases to describe and specify; to write poetry.
	4	Comprehension: To clarify the meanings of words, linking new meanings to known words.

STICK MAN

About the book

Stick Man by Julia Donaldson and illustrated by Axel Scheffler is a charming journey story about a Stick Man who, after going for a run one spring morning, gets taken miles from his home as a range of different people and animals mistake him for a useful stick. Each time he's picked up by someone, he reasserts his identity with a chorus of *I'm Stick Man, I'm Stick Man, I'm Stick Man, that's me*. Months later and miles from home, Stick Man is lying in a household grate when he hears Santa stuck in the chimney. He rescues Santa who in turn takes him home to his family in time for Christmas.

The easy rhythm and rhyme of the story make *Stick Man* ideal for reading aloud, with the children joining in with the chorus. Many children will be able to learn parts of the book by heart and create a dramatic retelling of the story. The clear setting and straightforward plot are ideal for teaching story elements and can lead to the children telling then writing their own version of the story. Discussions about prediction, cause and effect, what the children do at different times of the year such as, Christmas traditions in their family, should all be familiar enough to get most children talking.

Stick Man offers a wealth of learning opportunities across the curriculum. Alex Scheffler's charming illustrations capture Stick Man's journey through a very British countryside – parks, rivers, seaside, gardens and homes. As he travels, the seasons change from spring to summer, to autumn and winter, and different animals and activities can be seen in the background. These can link naturally to science activities around naming animals, locations, weather and the seasons. Craft activities following a woodland walk to collect sticks can include making a Stick Man, making woodland pictures or making decorations for the Christmas tree.

About the author

Julia Donaldson is best known for writing *The Gruffalo* and she spends much of her time performing musical versions of *The Gruffalo* and other stories around the country. Julia started writing poems, songs and plays as a child, performing them with her sister Mary. After university she wrote songs for children's television, one of which, *A Squash and a Squeeze*, became her first published book. Julia Donaldson was Children's Laureate from 2011 to 2013.

About the illustrator

Axel Scheffler has worked with Julia since the publication of *A Squash and a Squeeze*, but has worked on countless other titles, including his own pre-school 'Pip and Posy' books and Philip Ardagh's series 'The Grunts'. His distinctive characters and humorous detail are a perfect complement to Julia Donaldson's verse.

Key facts
Stick Man
Author: Julia Donaldson
Illustrator: Axel Scheffler
First published: 2009 by Alison Green Books
Did you know? The Stick Man character first appears in the hand of the Gruffalo's child in *The Gruffalo's Child*. A 2015 film of *Stick Man* starred Martin Freeman as Stick Man and Hugh Bonneville as Santa.

GUIDED READING

First reading

Look together at the cover of the book and read the title. Point to the character of Stick Man and establish that he looks just like a stick. Read the quotation on the back cover and locate Stick Man's wife and children. Read question 1 on the Guided Reading bookmark (page 10) and ask the children to discuss it with a partner.

Read the story aloud with drama (particularly for the '*Stick Man, oh Stick Man, beware of the …*' lines), encouraging the children to join in with the chorus. Pause at the point when Stick Man is lying in the grate and ask the children to discuss question 2 on the Guided Reading bookmark. Ask: *How will he be rescued?* Discuss the children's ideas, encouraging them to expand on them as much as possible.

Read to the end then ask the children to recap on the story. Read out question 3 on the bookmark and ask them to discuss this with a partner. After they've shared some ideas, ask: *How did Stick Man get so lost? Why did people take Stick Man?* Agree that because Stick Man looks like a stick he was picked up and used as a stick. Ask: *How does he finally get home?* (He rescues Santa when he got stuck up the chimney and Santa takes him back to his family tree.) If it is near Christmas (or maybe even if it is not) start up a rousing rendition of 'When Santa Got Stuck Up the Chimney.' Finally, ask the children to answer question 4 on the bookmark.

....

Second reading: Finding clues

Ask the children to look again at the cover. Ask: *Who wrote the story? Who drew the illustrations?* Point out that Axel Scheffler's illustrations add further information and atmosphere to the story as we see the journey that Stick Man goes on through the countryside and through the year.

Ask: *What time of year is it when Stick Man goes for his run?* The children might say Christmas because of the snowy cover and Santa at the end, but ask them to turn to the first spread of the story. Help them to see that it is spring, and point out the leaf buds and the blossom on the trees. Explain that the bluebells and tulips seen in the illustrations are spring flowers.

Focus on spread 3 and ask someone who has played Pooh-sticks to explain the rules of the game. (The players stand on a bridge over a flowing river – looking upstream – and simultaneously throw a stick into the water. Everyone rushes to the other side of the bridge and the person whose stick appears first is the winner.) Turn the page and look at the sad sight of Stick Man floating downstream and then stuck in the nest. Ask: *How far is he from home now? Do you think his wife and children know he is gone yet?* Ask: *Can anyone name any plants and animals shown in the illustrations here and on the next spread?* Point out, on spread 4: dog, swan, birds (specifically heron and great crested grebe), frog, bulrushes, willow tree, cows, duck, and on spread 5: moorhens, frog (ask if they can spot his eyes poking above the water) and sheep. Re-read the line beginning *The nest is deserted…* and ask: *Why is Stick Man free at last at this point?* (The eggs have hatched and the nest is abandoned.) *What happens next?* (He's free but drifting out to sea.)

Turn to the page beginning *He tosses and turns…* and ask: *Where is Stick Man now?* (at the beach) *What seaside items can you spot?* (seaweed, lighthouse, boats, sailboard, bucket, spade, crab, suntan lotion, umbrellas, beach towels, shells) *Who else is fighting over a stick?* (The crab and the little girl.) Ask: *The story started in spring but what season is it now? How can we tell?* (We can tell it's summer because the weather is hot and many people are on holiday at the seaside.) *What other locations have we had so far in the story?* (park and river)

Discuss question 5 on the Guided Reading bookmark. The pace of the story changes on spread 7 (beginning *I'm not a mast…*). Point out how time passes from summer to late autumn quite quickly because lots of events happen here. This is why there are so many little pictures. Together discuss question 6 on the bookmark (the illustrations show

8 READ&RESPOND Stick Man

GUIDED READING

the seasons changing). Ask the children to locate Stick Man in each picture and then to spot what is happening to the trees and the weather. Turn the page to reveal that it is now winter. Ask: *How long has Stick Man been gone from the family tree?* (about six or seven months) *What clues do we have in the snowy picture on the following page that it's nearly Christmas?* (carol singers)

Turn to the spread showing Santa for the first time. Ask the children to discuss with a partner the answer to question 7 on the bookmark. Share the children's ideas and agree that it is because it's very surprising and dramatic – both for the reader and Stick Man. Ask: *How should we read this line?* (loudly and dramatically) Ask the children to point out other Christmas objects in this spread and the next (for example, Christmas cards, nuts, Christmas tree, presents, stockings, Santa's sleigh). Ask: *Who can spot a character from another book by Julia Donaldson?* (the Gruffalo, as a tree decoration) Allow time for the children to talk about their own Christmas traditions. Point out and enjoy the patterned language with 'Stuck Man' and 'Stick Man'.

Read the final two spreads. The focus of the story changes here from Stick Man to the family he left behind. Talk about why the children might particularly miss their father at Christmas and listen to any children talking about missing relatives at this time of year. Look together at the children's toys and what they're made out of then turn to the final happy reunion. Ask: *What do the Sticks use for chairs and a table?* Point out the holly and mistletoe and ask: *Who else lives in the family tree with the Sticks?* (bats)

Third reading: Rhythm and rhyme

Ask: *Is this a story or a poem?* Agree that it is a story but it rhymes like a poem. Explain that it also has a strong rhythm, or beat, and that the length of the lines match. Ask the children to carry out the task in question 8 on the Guided Reading bookmark in pairs. Share the pairs of words that the children have found, reading out the lines in question and agreeing whether they rhyme or not. If all the rhyming words have the same spelling pattern at the end, as a class go on a hunt for rhyming words with different spelling patterns at the end, for example, throw/go, me/tree, free/sea, foam/home, bow/no, scarf/laugh, close/doze, choir/fire, friend/end, snow/go, bed/overhead.

Point out that the other way in which *Stick Man* is like a poem is that it has chorus. Challenge the children to answer question 9 on the bookmark. Remember the repeated phrase together and point out the contraction in 'I'm' and 'that's'.

Fourth reading: General thoughts

As a group, discuss question 10 on the Guided Reading bookmark. Listen to the children's thoughts and talk about how the animals and children think they are using a stick not a man. Ask: *Does that mean that their actions don't matter?* Move on to discussing how Stick Man might feel after his adventure. Talk about question 11 on the bookmark. *Ask: How can he stop himself being taken by someone again?* Perhaps he could get a hat or a cape or paint himself red. Perhaps he could get a whistle to blow when he is in trouble.

Ask: *Will he have any happy memories?* Perhaps he might decide to take his children to the seaside, or to wait up and see Santa the following year.

Ask the children to discuss their final thoughts about the story – did they think it was a happy or a sad story? Ask them to think about question 12 on the bookmark then share their favourite part with the group.

SCHOLASTIC
READ & RESPOND
Bringing the best books to life in the classroom

Stick Man
by Julia Donaldson

Focus on…
Meaning

1. Who are the main characters in the story?
2. How does Stick Man escape from the grate?
3. How does Stick Man get so far from home?
4. When does Stick Man finally arrive home?

Focus on…
Organisation

5. Which spread has the most pictures? Why?
6. How do we know that Stick Man has been away from home for a long time?

SCHOLASTIC
READ & RESPOND
Bringing the best books to life in the classroom

Stick Man
by Julia Donaldson

Focus on…
Language and features

7. Why is the line, 'And Santa falls into the room with a thump!' written larger than the other words in the book?
8. Find two words in the book that rhyme. Are they spelled in the same way?
9. Close the book. What repeated phrase does Stick Man say?

Focus on…
Purpose, viewpoints and effects

10. Are the children and animals who take Stick Man bad to do so?
11. Do you think that Stick Man will ever go for a jog again?
12. What was your favourite part of the story? Why?

SHARED READING

Extract 1

- Display Extract 1 and read it together, emphasising the rhythm and rhyme. Clap out the rhythm together and ask volunteers to find words that rhyme. Discuss the spelling patterns in the rhyming words.
- Find and circle all the contractions in the text.
- This is the opening of the book – locate and circle the elements that will be repeated throughout the story: repeated phrases, repeated events. Chant the chorus.
- Ask: *What is the dog's favourite trick?* Find the phrases that are just repeated within this passage: 'stick', 'drop it', 'fetch it'. Discuss the repetitive nature of throwing a stick for an enthusiastic dog and how this has been captured here. Encourage the children to read the passage rhythmically.
- Ask: *Why is* 'Stick Man, oh Stick Man, beware of the dog' *written in italics?* (For example, because it encourages the reader to say the line dramatically, because the voice changes from telling the story to talking to Stick Man, because the event described is worrying and so on.)

Extract 2

- In this extract, Stick Man is lying in the fire. Point out that throughout the book Stick Man does not do much – he is carried from one place to another; all he can do is shout. Here, someone else is in trouble and Stick Man finally acts.
- Circle the phrase 'A Stuck Man...who could that be?' Find and circle all the clues that this is Santa. Ask: *How many letters do we need to change to turn 'Stick Man' into 'Stuck Man'?*
- Ask: *Why is the last line written so much larger than the rest of the text?* (To create drama, to make you shout when you read it, because it's so surprising.)
- Together find the words ending in 'le'. List other words ending in 'le' (puzzle, table, and so on).
- Circle the word 'scratch'. Discuss how the first three letters each make a phoneme but that 'tch' only makes one. Ask pairs to find all the clusters of two and three consonants and discuss the phonemes they represent.

Extract 3

- Read the text together. Pause on the word 'foraging' and ask a volunteer to attempt to read it, checking that they are reading it phonetically. Explain its meaning (to search for things that can be collected in the wild).
- Establish that this is an instruction text to make a Stick Man. Ask different children to locate and circle: heading, introduction, 'What you need' list, numbered instructions, diagrams, instruction words (go, choose, take), adverbs, and warning.
- Ask: *Why do we use 'bossy words'?* Find the verbs and talk about the forms, verbally replacing them with incorrect versions to highlight how verbs change.
- Ask pairs to discuss how they might make Stick Man's stick children three. Challenge more confident learners to discuss how they might make one of the children's toys. Tell them to use the format of Extract 3 to write a set of instructions for this. In a piece of shared writing, write a class set of instructions.

SHARED READING

Extract 1

Stick Man lives in the family tree
With his Stick Lady Love and their stick children three.

One day he wakes early and goes for a jog.
Stick Man, oh Stick Man, beware of the dog!

"A stick!" barks the dog. "An excellent stick!
The right kind of stick for my favourite trick.

"I'll fetch it and drop it, and fetch it – and then
"I'll drop it and fetch it and drop it again."

"I'm not a stick! Why can't you see,
I'm Stick Man, *I'm Stick Man,*
I'M STICK MAN, that's me,
And I want to go home to the family tree!"

SHARED READING

Extract 2

He dreams of his kids and his Stick Lady Love,

Then suddenly wakes.
What's that noise up above?
It starts as a chuckle,
then turns to a shout:
"Oh-ho-ho-ho-ho . . . I'm STUCK!
Get me OUT!"

A Stuck Man? *A Stuck Man?*
Now who could that be?
"Don't worry!" cries Stick Man.
"I'll soon set you free."

A scratch and a scrape and
a flurry of soot.
A wiggle, a jiggle, and –
out pokes a foot!
A shove and a nudge,
a hop and a jump . . .

And Santa falls into the room with a thump!

▼ SHARED READING

Extract 3

How to make a Stick Man and his Stick Lady Love

Go on a foraging walk in the woods and use your finds to make a Stick Man and his Stick Lady Love.

You will need:
- sticks
- small berries
- googly eyes
- glue
- tiny and small leaves
- thin garden wire

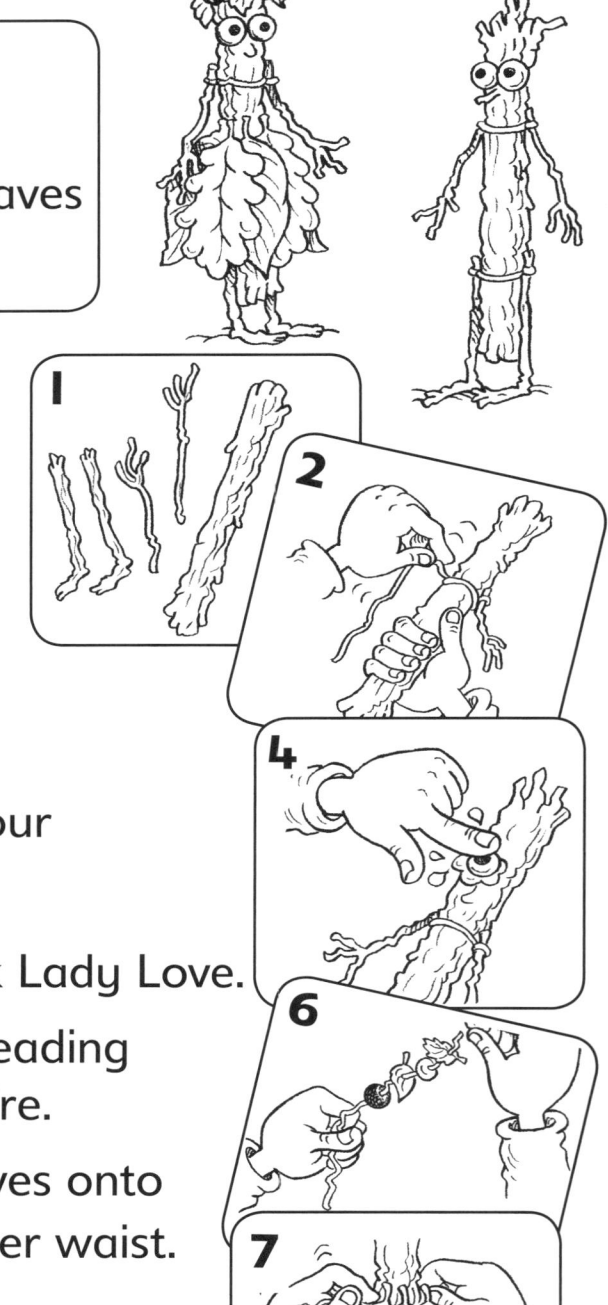

1. Choose a stick for Stick Man's body and four smaller sticks to use for his arms and legs.
2. Wind garden wire around one arm, then around the body and then around the second arm.
3. Do the same to attach the legs.
4. Glue on googly eyes to complete your Stick Man.
5. Repeat steps 1 to 3 to create a Stick Lady Love.
6. Make a garland for her head by threading tiny leaves and berries on garden wire.
7. Make a skirt by threading small leaves onto wire and then wrapping it around her waist.

Safety: Wire can be sharp! Ask an adult to help you cut it to the right length.

PHONICS & SPELLING

1. Spelling /k/

Objective
To learn 'ck' and 'k' spellings for the /k/ sound.

What you need
Copies of *Stick Man*, printable page 'Spelling /k/', paper, glue.

What to do

- Ask the children to suggest words with the /k/ sound. Write these on the board clustering them into the different spelling options (for example, cat, cream, case; click, rack, pick; bake, hike, poke).

- Provide printable page 'Spelling /k/', paper, glue and copies of *Stick Man* to pairs of children. Challenge the children to find each word in the book.

- Ask the pairs to cut out and stick down their words into three lists: 'c' spelling, 'k' spelling, 'ck' spelling. When they've finished ask them to look at each list – and the list of words on the board – to see if they can see any patterns.

- Share the children's ideas and agree that: 'c' is used for the /k/ sound at beginning of words; 'ck' is the most common spelling at the end of a word after a short vowel sound; 'k' is used when the next letter is 'i' or 'e' (or 'y'); 'k' is used after 'oo'.

Differentiation
Support: Focus on locating the /k/ sound in the words and sorting them into 'c', 'k' and 'ck' piles.
Extension: Challenge children to find two words in *Stick Man* where the /k/ sound is spelt 'ch' (Christmas, choir). Challenge them to find three words where the letter 'c' is used for the /s/ sound (face, race, voice).

2. Adding endings – changing words

Objective
To find root words and use 'ing', 'ed', 'er', and 'est' endings.

What you need
Copies of *Stick Man*, interactive activity 'Adding endings'.

What to do

- Ask the children to tell you all the things that Stick Man does, or that happen to him, for example, goes jogging, floats down the river and so on.

- As the children make their suggestions, write the verb on the board, surreptitiously changing its form so that it is either ending in 's', 'ing' or 'ed', and making simpler choices for younger children, for example, jogging or jogs, floating, helps, throws, fetched, chuckling or chuckles, dozes or dozed, building.

- Ask pairs of children to work using their whiteboards to write the words and draw a line between the root word and the suffix. Remind older children that the root word will have been changed and will look slightly odd in some words.

- Carry out the interactive activity 'Adding endings'.

Differentiation
Support: Create word cards and endings for the root words suggested in the shared activity. Choose root words that do not require changes when the endings are added. Ask children to make words using all the different endings.
Extension: Ask children to create a set of word sentences for their partner to solve.

PHONICS & SPELLING

3. Collect them all!

Objective
To learn new ways of spelling phonemes for which one or more spellings are already known.

What you need
Printable pages 'Collect them all', copies of *Stick Man*.

What to do

- Using the phoneme you are focusing on at the moment, ask the children to tell you the main spelling options for the phoneme. Repeat with other phonemes, such as the long vowel phonemes. Slip in the phonemes on thr printable pages 'Collect them all!' (/ee/, /oi/, /ur/, /or/, /o/, /u/, /i/).

- Hand out copies of the printable pages 'Collect them all' and ask the children to race their partner to find an example of each phoneme-grapheme correspondence in *Stick Man*. Share the words the children have found, for example, family, chimney, sea; me, voice, boys; girl, turn, deserted; warm, laugh, love. There is more than one option for some of the answers.

Differentiation

Support: Practise the phonemes with the children beforehand and only ask them to complete the first printable page. You could also provide the learners with the words on cards for them to match against the printable sheets (rather than finding them in the book).

Extension: Challenge early finishers to use their reading book – or any other books in the classroom – to find another word for each phoneme card on the printable pages.

4. Contraction pairs

Objective
To read and learn to spell words with contracted forms.

What you need
Extract 1, printable page 'Contraction pairs' (two copies for each pair), scissors.

What to do

- Display Extract 1 and read the chorus together. Circle the words *I'm* and *that's* and ask the children to tell you the long versions of these words. Write 'I am' and 'that is' next to the words.

- Invite children to come forward and circle a contraction, then attempt to write the long version alongside it.

- Provide the printable page 'Contraction pairs'. Ask the children to cut out the pairs of words and fold and stick them to create flash cards for each contraction. They can then use the flash cards to test each other on reading and spelling the contractions.

- Provide new copies of the printable page 'Contraction pairs', cut up into individual cards. Ask the pairs to use the cards to play 'Contractions Pairs' – taking turns to turn over cards to find a pair (one long and one contracted version creating the pair).

- Find the words in *Stick Man* and read the lines with the long versions. Establish that it doesn't sound as good.

Differentiation

Support: Focus on reading the words. Ask children to pair up the long and contracted versions.

Extension: Ask children to create more cards for the game of pairs, finding other contractions.

PLOT, CHARACTER & SETTING

1. A series of unfortunate events

Objective
To discuss the significance of the title and the events. To discuss the sequence of events in books that are structured in different ways.

What you need
Copies of *Stick Man*, photocopiable page 20 'A series of unfortunate events', scissors, paper, glue, interactive activity 'Ordering Stick Man', copies of *Unfortunately* by Alan Durant (Extension only).

What to do
- Provide photocopiable page 20 'A series of unfortunate events'. Ask the children if they think that 'A series of unfortunate events' might have been a good title for *Stick Man*.
- Ask pairs of children to cut out the individual event cards and to stick them down in the correct order on a piece of paper.
- Next, ask them to draw a happy face or a sad face by each event to indicate whether it is a good or a bad thing that has happened to Stick Man.
- Ask: *Do more good things or bad things happen to Stick Man?* (more bad things) Ask: *Is it a sad book?* (Agree that it is happy at the end but it is very sad when he is on the fire and his family is missing him.) Ask: *Are any of the good things so good that they balance out the book and make it happy?*

Differentiation
Support: Ask children to do interactive activity 'Ordering Stick Man'.
Extension: Help more confident learners to see *Stick Man* as a series of small events. Ask them to read *Unfortunately* by Alan Durant or another book with a similar plot and compare the stories.

2. All because of the dog

Objective
To use subordination (when, if, that, or because) and coordination (or, and, but).

What you need
Photocopiable page 21 'All because of the dog', a bag.

What to do
- Ask the children some quiz questions about the cause of the events of the plot, for example: *How does Stick Man get to the beach? Why is Stick Man on the fire? How does Stick Man get home?* Encourage children to create whole-sentence answers, for example, 'When the nest is empty Stick Man drifts down the river.'.
- Write the words 'when', 'that', 'because' and 'but' on the board and explain how these words can be used to tell the reader more information about an event, for example, why it happened.
- Create flashcards from photocopiable page 21 'All because of the dog' and put them in a bag. Ask volunteers to take out a word and make up a sentence about Stick Man using the word, for example:
  - The dog picked up Stick Man because he thought he was a stick.
  - Stick Man woke up when he heard someone shouting.
  - Stick Man started to run home but a girl picked him up.
- Ask the children to carry out the activity on the photocopiable sheet. Share the sentences and point out the extra information introduced.

Differentiation
Support: Provide a scribe for these children and ask them to focus on creating sentences for 'because', 'and' and 'but'.
Extension: Challenge early finishers to write a sentence for 'if'.

READ&RESPOND Stick Man **17**

PLOT, CHARACTER & SETTING

3. How did that make you feel?

Objectives
To make inferences on the basis of what is being said and done. To use subordination (when, if that or because) and coordination (or, and but).

What you need
Copies of *Stick Man*; printable pages 'How did they feel?'

What to do
- Organise the children into pairs and provide copies of *Stick Man*. Ask the pairs to go through the book, a page at a time, pointing to the characters and saying how they think they feel, for example, Stick Man and his family are happy playing in the tree; Stick Man is scared of the dog.
- Provide printable pages 'How did they feel?' and ask the children to write a phrase or a sentence about how the character feels in the situations given. Challenge older children to use 'when' or 'because' in their sentences, for example, Stick Man is lonely when he thinks of his family. The boy is happy because he has found a stick for his snowman.
- Share the sentences together and work as a class to improve each one with more interesting emotion words.

Differentiation
Support: Provide children with emotion words for them to stick on the printable sheets: happy, excited, scared, lonely, angry, cross, relieved.
Extension: Ask children to write sentences about other points in the story.

4. Where did he go?

Objective
To discuss the sequence of events in books that are structured in different ways.

What you need
Copies of *Stick Man*, individual whiteboards, interactive activity 'Stick Man's journey'.

Cross-curricular link
Geography

What to do
- Ask the children to work in pairs and give each pair a copy of *Stick Man*. Ask them to list on their individual whiteboards, all the places that Stick Man goes to on his journey: park, river, riverbank, seaside, pavement, house, tree.
- Look at the first images of the park, the river, the seaside and the snow-covered park and ask the children to tell you the activities, animals and plants that they can see in each. In a piece of shared writing, write some descriptive sentences about each location, for example: A swan carefully makes a nest near the bulrushes. The sweet-singing choir stand under the lamp post.
- Ask the children to complete interactive activity 'Stick Man's journey' which requires them to label some geographical features and ask them to say what happened at each point.
- Display the completed screen from the interactive activity and ask volunteers to use it to tell parts of the story, remembering the chorus and any other favourite lines.

Differentiation
Support: Re-read the story with the children, pointing out each area and its features ahead of carrying out the interactive activity.
Extension: Ask children to write their own descriptive sentences.

PLOT, CHARACTER & SETTING

5. Animal I spy

Objective
To draw on what they already know or on background information and vocabulary provided by the teacher.

What you need
Copies of *Stick Man*, printable page 'Animal I spy', media resource 'Animal photographs', interactive activity 'What's the animal?'.

Cross-curricular links
Science, art and design

What to do

- Ask: *What animals are there in* Stick Man*?* Most children will remember the dog but can they remember any other animals from the illustrations?

- Provide the printable page 'Animal I spy' and have a race (if appropriate) to see who can find all the animals in *Stick Man*.

- Share the locations in the book together and read the names of the animals from the printable page – reminding the children to use their phonics knowledge to attempt to read the trickier names. Look at the photographs of the animals in the media resource 'Animal photographs'. Click on the photograph to reveal the name of the animal.

- Explain that most of *Stick Man* takes place in parks near a town. Tell them that many of these animals are quite common near towns and that they should be able to spot one or two as they go out and about. (Explain that some, such as the red squirrel, may not live in their area.)

- Create a 'Stick Man park' background and ask the children to paint one animal from the list and add it to the display.

Differentiation
Support: Direct children to the best pages to search on.
Extension: Ask early finishers to carry out interactive activity 'What's the animal?'.

6. Spring, summer, autumn, winter

Objective
To make inferences on the basis of what is being said and done.

What you need
Copies of *Stick Man*, media resource 'Trees through the seasons', four flipchart-sized pieces of paper.

Cross-curricular link
Science

What to do

- Show the images of apple trees through the year from the media resource 'Trees through the seasons' and ask the children to tell you what happens to the tree in each season.

- Provide copies of *Stick Man*. Ask: *When does the story of Stick Man take place?*

- Together, look through the book and agree that Stick Man goes for a run in spring and gets home on Christmas Eve. Remember the months of the year and work out that Stick Man is away from home for about seven months.

- Head the pieces of paper 'Spring', 'Summer', 'Autumn' and 'Winter' and place them around the classroom. Organise the class into four groups and ask them to rotate around the four sheets, writing two events from *Stick Man* on each sheet (without repeating events). Point out that the task will get harder.

- Discuss how the children knew what happened when (from the illustrations). Ask the children what they do in each season (for example, Sports Day, holiday, back to school, Halloween, Christmas, their birthday and so on).

Differentiation
Support: Provide images for children to stick on to the flipchart.
Extension: Ask children to scribe for their group.

▼ PLOT, CHARACTER & SETTING

A series of unfortunate events

- Lots of dreadful things happen to Stick Man. Cut out these event cards and put the events in order.
- Decide if they are good events or bad events and add a smiley face or a sad face.

Stick Man rescues Santa from the chimney.	○
A dog takes Stick Man.	○
The park closes and Stick Man is free.	○
Stick Man is used for Pooh-sticks.	○
Stick Man is used for a sandcastle.	○
Santa takes Stick Man home to his family.	○
Stick Man goes for a jog.	○
The eggs hatch and Stick Man is free of the nest.	○
Stick Man is used as an arm for a snowman.	○
Stick Man is put on the fire.	○
Stick Man is used by a swan for a nest.	○
The fire is not lit.	○
The snowman melts and Stick Man is free.	○

PLOT, CHARACTER & SETTING

All because of the dog

- Explain more about what happens to Stick Man by writing a sentence about *Stick Man* using each of these words.

READ&RESPOND Stick Man 21

TALK ABOUT IT

1. Tell me a story

Objective
To retell the story. To give well-structured descriptions, explanations and narratives for different purposes.

What you need
Copies of *Stick Man*.

What to do
- Tell the children that they are going to be telling their own version of *Stick Man*, re-reading the story then drawing a story map to help them with their retelling.
- Provide pairs of children with copies of *Stick Man* and ask them to read it to each other. Draw a winding path on the board and draw Stick Man and his family at the top, then start drawing scenes from the story down the path – for example, a jogging Stick Man and the dog.
- Ask the children to draw their own simple story map for *Stick Man*. Tell them to choose only four things that Stick Man is used for.
- Ask them to use their maps to work on a retelling of the story, first telling the story to themselves, then to another classmate. Encourage them to use the chorus from the book.
- Ask volunteers to tell their story to the class, encouraging the rest of the class to join in with the chorus.

Differentiation
Support: Ask the children to focus on just the first half of the book.
Extension: Encourage children to use their voices in different ways when retelling their story.

2. I'm not a football!

Objective
To maintain attention and participate actively in collaborative conversations, staying on topic and initiating and responding to comments.

What you need
A range of sticks, stones, pine cones, leaves.

Cross-curricular link
PSHE

What to do
- If possible, go on a foraging walk to collect sticks, stones, pine cones, leaves and any other useful objects you find.
- Give small mixed-ability groups an object each. Tell them that as a group they need to think of as many uses as they can for it. Remind them of all the things that Stick Man was used for and demonstrate with a stone, pondering that it could be a paperweight, a football, a necklace, a marker for hopscotch and so on. Model discussing the features of the stone that make it suitable for its different purposes.
- Set the class to their discussion reminding them of their group discussion skills.
- Swap objects amongst the groups until each group has had each type of object.
- Share the children's ideas, drawing out their thoughts with further questioning. Praise children whom you heard asking questions and building on other children's ideas in the group work.

Differentiation
Support: Spend some time before the session talking about what the objects could be to give children the confidence to talk clearly in the group.
Extension: Ask children to ensure that everyone is getting a chance to speak and be listened to.

TALK ABOUT IT

3. Stick Man song

Objective
To participate in discussions, performances, role play and improvisations.

What you need
Printable pages 'Stick Man song', craft materials (paper, paints and lollipop sticks).

Cross-curricular link
Music

What to do

- Display the printable pages 'Stick Man song' and read it together. Find the passages that are similar to the book and those that are different. Explore how the story has been condensed.
- Ask: *Which events have been included?* (For example, the dog, Pooh-sticks, the swan, the sandcastle, the bag, the sword for a knight, the snowman, the fire and Santa.)
- Read the words a few times so the children are very familiar with the song, and learn the chorus off by heart.
- Listen to the song, encouraging the children to join in.
- Provide craft materials and ask the children to create a character of their choice from the song on a lollipop stick. Sing the song again, asking the children to stand up and wave their lollipop stick character and say the words that character says at relevant points. The children will need to remember to be quiet for the parts where another character is speaking or singing but will need to remember to join in with such lines as 'yells a dad'.

Differentiation
Support: Provide percussion instruments for children who are not confident singers.
Extension: Ask more confident singers to take on a solo line.

4. Off by heart

Objective
To participate in performances, role play and improvisations.

What you need
Copies of *Stick Man*, internet access, the film *A Stick Family Christmas*.

What to do

- Work as a class to create a performance of *Stick Man*. If possible, search online for the trailer for Scamp Theatre's production of *Stick Man* and watch this to get some ideas before starting out.
- As a class create a cast list and allocate parts – doubling up where necessary and allowing each animal including swan chicks to have a role. Provide each child with a copy of the book and ask them to write down what they want to say – telling them it can be one word or a whole sentence depending on what they think is needed. Tell them that if their character has spoken lines in the book, they should copy those out.
- Organise the children into scenes and encourage them to help each other improve what they want to say. Encourage them to improvise their actions but choosing and sticking to a final option.
- Take on the role of narrator and organise the characters into a play including a rendition of the Stick Man song.
- Make masks for the characters and a backdrop.
- After your performance, watch the BBC film adaptation of Stick Man – *A Stick Family Christmas* and compare performances.

Differentiation
Support: Ask children to take on the role of the animals and give them group lines to say.
Extension: Ask confident learners to take on the role of the narrator or Stick Man.

TALK ABOUT IT

5. That's not fair!

Objective
To articulate and justify answers, arguments and opinions. To consider and evaluate different viewpoints, attending to and building on the contributions of others.

What you need
Photocopiable page 25 'That's not fair!'

What to do
- Ask: *Was the girl who took Stick Man for Pooh-sticks cruel?* Listen to the children's ideas and then play devil's advocate: If she had been more thoughtful she would have looked at him and seen it was a man or heard him crying and so on.
- Organise the children into mixed-ability discussion groups and provide copies of the photocopiable page 25 'That's not fair!'. Ask the children to discuss each statement in turn, deciding as a group whether or not they agree with the statement. Read the objectives together and recap on group discussion rules.
- Encourage the children to spend about five minutes on each statement, thinking of all the different angles and resisting the temptation to make a snap decision. Remind the children that, if there is a difference of opinion in the group, they should respectfully try to change each other's minds.
- Afterwards, debate each statement, listening and extending the various views.

Differentiation
Support: Helping them to articulate ideas on two or three statements.
Extension: Place each statement in the middle of a flipchart and ask the children to write 'Agree' or 'Disagree' with supporting statements. Challenge children to argue against their previous views.

6. Seasonal presentation

Objective
To participate in presentations.

What you need
Copies of *Stick Man*; individual whiteboards.

Cross-curricular link
Science

What to do
- Recap on how the seasons change in *Stick Man* (see page 19).
- Provide groups of four children with four individual whiteboards each, headed with the names of the seasons.
- Ask the groups to draw or write four things for each season (using *Stick Man* for ideas). Tell them to think about trees, weather, activities, festivals and so on.
- Pause and share the children's ideas so far, for example, spring – blossom, Easter, warm, pond dipping, first flowers, plant seeds; summer – green trees, end of school, holidays, hot, beach; autumn – leaves turn different colours, windy, Halloween, football; winter – bare trees, cold, snow, rain, Christmas, nativity play.
- When the groups are ready, ask them to choose their favourite four ideas, using ideas from the other groups if they like. Explain that they can either present one season each, or can each say one thing each about each season (for example, one child could talk about what the trees are doing, another about festivals, another about sports and another about school activities).
- Share the presentations.

Differentiation
Support: Provide children with pictures to sort into the different seasons.
Extension: Challenge children to create their own presentations using a presentation package or drawing their own images.

TALK ABOUT IT

That's not fair!

- Cut out these statements about Stick Man.
- Read them. Do you agree with them?
- Organise them into piles of 'I agree' and 'I don't agree'.

Stick Man should never leave the tree again.	Stick Man should have talked to the people who took him.
The dog was wrong to take Stick Man.	Santa should have taken Stick Man straight home.
Stick Lady Love should have gone to find Stick Man.	Stick Man should have escaped from the nest earlier.
Stick Man is very unlucky.	

GET WRITING

1. Stone Boy that's me!

Objective

To punctuate sentences using a capital letter and a full stop, question mark or exclamation mark. To use sentences with different forms. To use expanded noun phrases.

What you need

A stone with a face drawn on it ('Stone Boy').

What to do

- Introduce Stone Boy and tell the class that he lives in a pile of stones by a gate to the park with eight Stone brothers. (*Stone Boy lived in a pile by a gate* or *With his Stone Mummy dear and his stone brothers eight.*)

- Tell the children that one day Stone Boy's mum sent him out to get some moss to make a bed for his grandmother who was coming to stay. On his way back some boys use him as a football. Ask: *What do you think Stone Man said?* (For example, *I'm Stone Man, and it's getting so dark. I've got to get back to the gate in the park.*)

- Ask: *What else might have happened to Stone Boy?* Recap on ideas from 'I'm not a football!' on page 22. Ask: *How will he be rescued?* Perhaps a walker picks him up and drops him back home. Perhaps he also rescues Santa.

- Tell the children to create a storyboard for their own story of Stone Boy, writing a punctuated caption for each picture, including one caption that is a question, and one that is an exclamation.

- Ask early finishers to revisit each caption and try to add one adjective to each one.

Differentiation

Support: Draft out the story together and provide vocabulary on cards.
Extension: Expect children to create a story with more of their own detail.

2. Stick Man's child

Objectives

To write a short narrative.
To write narratives about personal experiences and those of others.

What you need

Copies of *Stick Man*, *The Gruffalo* and *The Gruffalo's Child* by Julia Donaldson and Axel Scheffler, photocopiable page 29 'Stick Man's child'.

Cross-curricular link

Art and design

What to do

- Read *The Gruffalo* and *The Gruffalo's Child* by Julia Donaldson. Explain that the Gruffalo's child manages to trick the mouse.

- Tell the children that they are going to be writing a sequel to *Stick Man* in which the Stick Man's daughter goes on an adventure and meets some of the same characters but gets away each time and is home for tea.

- Provide copies of photocopiable page 29 'Stick Man's child'. Ask the children to talk about what is happening in each picture and decide what Stick Man's child might be saying. Point out the noun phrases and tell the children that phrases like this will make their writing more interesting.

- Ask the children to take turns telling the story to each other creating one sentence for each picture using the noun phrases and creating some dialogue for the Stick Man's child.

- When they are ready, ask the children to write a short version of their story, using phonics to attempt to spell words. Tell them to check their story for capital letters and full stops.

Differentiation

Support: Ask children to work on an oral telling of their story; scribe this story for them.
Extension: Confident learners should attempt to include some further adjectives in the story.

GET WRITING

3. Visit Beacon Park

Objectives
To write for different purposes. To write down ideas and/or key words, including new vocabulary.

What you need
Individual whiteboards, A3 pieces of paper, media resource 'Animal photographs'.

Cross-curricular link
Science

What to do

- Tell the children that they are going to be creating an information poster for the park in *Stick Man*. Ask: *What do you like to do at the park?* Tell the children to turn to a partner and say why they should go to your local park. Listen to the children's sentences and model how to turn these into an introduction to the park. For example, 'Visit Beacon Park: you can play games, eat lunch and spot animals.'
- Model how to revisit sentences to add adjectives to create noun phrases. For example, 'At Beacon Park you can play sporty games, eat delicious food and spot busy animals.'
- Model planning your poster. Say: *I'm going to write my sentence here, I'm going to put a map or picture of the park here. This side of the poster is going to show all the animals in the park and their names.*
- Ask the children to plan their poster on their whiteboards.
- Go through media resource 'Animal photographs' to explain all the possible animals they might find in the park.
- Provide large pieces of paper for the children and give them time to create their poster.

Differentiation
Support: Create an introductory sentence in a piece of shared writing.
Extension: Encourage children to write a sentence about the sports activities.

4. I'm Little Red

Objective
To write poetry.

What you need
A version of 'The Gingerbread Man', a range of fairy tales that the children are familiar with.

Cross-curricular link
Music

What to do

- Tell the story of 'The Gingerbread Man' and ask the children to join in with the chorus:
 Run, run as fast as you can
 You can't catch me
 I'm the Gingerbread Man.
- Write the chorus on the board and circle the rhymes. Clap along with the rhythm.
- Compare the two stories: point out that unlike Stick Man, the Gingerbread Man escapes everyone but then meets a soggy end.
- Ask the children to think of other repeated phrases in fairy tales, for example, 'Jack and the Beanstalk' and 'Three Little Pigs'.
- In a piece of shared writing, create a chorus for Little Red Riding Hood to say, for example:
 Skip, skip, skip – I'm Little Red
 And I'm off to visit my Grandma in bed.
- Challenge the children, working in pairs, to create a rhyming couplet that the wolf could say. Then ask them to choose another fairy tale, for example 'Cinderella', 'Sleeping Beauty', 'Robin Hood', and write a chorus for it. Remove the need to rhyme if necessary.
- Share the children's ideas, writing them on the board and chanting them together, rhythmically as a class.

Differentiation
Support: Carry out this activity as a piece of shared writing.
Extension: Encourage children to create a chorus that rhymes and scans.

GET WRITING

5. How to make a pine-cone fairy

Objectives

To compose a sentence orally before writing it.

What you need

Extract 3 (page 14), media resource 'Pine-cone creations', photocopiable page 30 'How to make a pine-cone fairy', a range of sticks, leaves, pine cones, acorns, acorn cups, googly eyes, pipe cleaners, paper, glue, wooden beads, pom-poms.

Cross-curricular link

Design and technology

What to do

- Display Extract 3 and circle the features of an instruction text.
- Display the photographs from media resource 'Pine-cone creations' and discuss how they might have been made.
- Display photocopiable page 30 'How to make a pine-cone fairy'. Together, create a 'What we need' list: pine cone, pipe cleaners, an acorn cup, wooden bead, leaves, glue. Then write a set of instructions for making the fairy.
- Provide a wide range of foraged and craft materials and ask the children to design and make some model animals or toys.
- Ask them to choose their best and provide a partner with the materials needed to make another one and tell them how to make it, with their partner following their instructions.
- Ask the children to draw and write instructions for how to make their model.

Differentiation

Support: Make a simple pine-cone hedgehog with the children. Provide word and phrase cards for them to use to write simple instructions.
Extension: Expect children to add adverbs to their instructions.

6. Stick Man game

Objective

To re-read what they have written to check it makes sense.
To check that verbs are used correctly and consistently.

What you need

Copies of *Stick Man*, printable page 'Stick Man game instructions', printable page 'Stick Man game' (enlarged to A3), playing card sized paper, dice.

What to do

- Display an enlarged version of printable page 'Stick Man game instructions' and read the instructions together.
- Explain to the children that they have to write the 'Stick Man beware!' cards. These cards should be a mixture of good and bad events (for example, You are used for Pooh-sticks – go back to the trap; A dog plays fetch with you – miss a turn; You escape the nest – go forward 10 spaces; You meet Santa – take your counter to the family tree.).
- Organise the children into pairs to write their cards, re-reading and checking the verbs make sense as 'you' verbs. Ask the children to swap cards with another pair to check for mistakes. Allow them to use any ideas and create a few more cards.
- Give each pair a die and copies of the printable page. Ask the children to cut out the counters, colour them different colours and play their game from printable page 'Stick Man game'.

Differentiation

Support: Provide a scribe so children can concentrate on orally creating sentences.
Extension: Ask children to create events that are not in the book for their game.

GET WRITING

Stick Man's child

- Stick Man's child goes on her own adventure to the park.
- Write something she says in the speech bubbles.

Stick Man's child skips.

A stick for my game!

Sharp bop!

Pooh-stick!

Clever jump

For my nest.

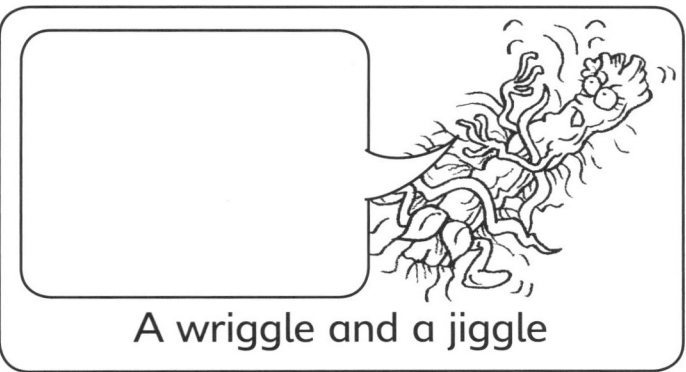

A wriggle and a jiggle

▼ GET WRITING

How to make a pine-cone fairy

- Complete these instructions for how to make a fairy.

What you need:

_____

_____

_____

_____

ASSESSMENT

1. Reordering Stick Man

Objective
To sequence sentences to form short narratives. To use subordination and coordination.

What you need
Interactive activities 'Ordering Stick Man' and 'Stick Man captions'.

What to do
- Ask the children how well they remember *Stick Man*. Ask the children to carry out interactive activity 'Ordering Stick Man', individually. This activity asks the children to put the events that happen in the story in sequence order.
- They can then move on to interactive activity 'Stick Man captions'. Tell the children that their main task is to write a caption that has a capital letter and a full stop.
- Next, challenge them to try to add some lines that they remember from the book to their sentences. Can they add in the chorus?
- Finally, ask the children to attempt to add one question to their captions – this could be one they remember from the story (for example, Can anyone wake him, before it's too late?).
- Challenge children to use the words 'because' and 'when' at least once to show their understanding of why things happened.
- When the children have finished their captions, ask them to check by reading them aloud to themselves. Ask: *Do they sound right? Do all the verbs match across the story – or do they move between past and present?*

Differentiation
Support: Ask children to order the picture then write key words in the space for captions.
Extension: Challenge children to write a series of captions that would tell the story without the images.

2. Contraction practice

Objective
To read and spell words with contracted forms.

What you need
Interactive activity 'Contraction practice', copies of *Stick Man*, printable page 'Contraction pairs'.

What to do
- Ask the children to write down the chorus from *Stick Man*. When they've finished, ask them to circle the contractions.
- Hand out copies of *Stick Man* and ask the children to use it in pairs to test each other on contractions. They should take turns to read out a contraction from the book while the other writes it down.
- Finally, ask the children to do interactive activity 'Contraction practice'. In this activity the children listen to a range of contractions. The first part of the activity requires them to click on the correct answer; the screen 4 requires them to listen to a word and type it.
- Afterwards, share the examples that the children find hard to remember.

Differentiation
Support: Ask children to revisit printable page 'Contraction pairs' and play pairs again until they are very familiar with the pairings.
Extension: Ask children to create the longest list of contractions they can, finding them in books around the classroom and then, when they've exhausted those, on the internet.

ASSESSMENT

3. Scorching summer poem

Objective
To write poetry using expanded noun phrases.

What you need
Media resource 'Trees through the seasons'.

Cross-curricular link
Science

What to do
- Display the photographs from the media resource 'Trees through the seasons'. Tell the children that you want them to write a list poem about the seasons – writing one verse for each season. Tell them that each line of the poem should be a different expanded noun phrase.
- Model writing some ideas for spring. First draw up a list of nouns that conjure spring: blossom, chocolate, buds on the trees, splashing in puddles, playing outside at last, daffodils, rabbits coming out of hibernation and so on. Demonstrate adding an adjective to each to create the list poem: frothy blossom, gooey chocolate, tight buds, welly boots, outside play, bright daffodils, sleepy rabbits and so on.
- Create noun lists for each season on the board – or in pairs if more appropriate.
- Tell the children to work individually to create their poems about seasons. Encourage them to revisit their lists after a first draft and revise the order and improve on any adjectives.
- Ask the children to add a title for each verse, for example, Fresh spring, Lazy summer, Crisp autumn, Wonderful winter. Ask them to use their best handwriting to create a display of their poems.

Differentiation
Support: Provide a word bank of nouns and adjectives for children to combine to create one verse about a favourite season.
Extension: Expect children to create their poems by creating their own lists of nouns first, rather than waiting for a class list.

4. Vocabulary match

Objective
To discuss the meaning of new words.

What you need
Printable page 'Vocabulary match'.

What to do
- Remind the children that over the course of the unit they have practised reading and writing the names of plants, animals and geography features.
- Hand out printable page 'Vocabulary match' and ask the children to match up the words to their meanings.
- Next, ask the children to write sentences for five of the words, remembering for each sentence to include a capital letter and a full stop. Challenge them to use one adjective in each sentence. Explain that the sentences can be stories, silly, sensible or descriptive, but they have to use the word correctly. For example: I put out bread for the hungry blue tit. Paul slipped off the riverbank into the freezing water. The blackbird has a yellow beak.
- Share the sentences between partners, checking each other's spelling, adjectives and use of the words.

Differentiation
Support: Practise reading the words together, discussing the meaning. Create sentences together as a shared task.
Extension: Challenge children to use the word 'because' or 'when' in two of the sentences.

32 READ&RESPOND Stick Man